GENTLEMAN AT LARGE

Gentleman At Large is the first published collection of poems by Charles Evans. His new collection brings together poems, written over a period of twenty years, which have won numerous national and international awards.

In 2005 Charles Evans was awarded a Hawthornden Fellowship for poetry. Brian Patten said of him that *'there is a clarity that marks him out as a true poet.'*

Alan Brownjohn commented: Charles Evans' poems *'can be gritty and truthful, or show a flair for fantasy and sly wit, especially in dealing with public themes.'*

The collection ranges in subject from illness to health, from politics to pornography and from God to infidelity.

GENTLEMAN AT LARGE

Charles Evans

www.realpress.co.uk

First published in Great Britain in 2010 by

www.realpress.co.uk

Real Press is part of Real Group (UK) Limited
Canterbury Innovation Centre
University Road
Canterbury
CT2 7FG
UK
www.realpress.co.uk

FIRST EDITION

British Library Cataloguing in Publication Data
a catalogue record of this publication is available
from the British Library.

ISBN: 978-0-9564127-1-3

Dust jacket design by Katherine Boyes

Printed and bound in the UK by the MPG Books Group, Bodmin and King's Lynn

ACKNOWLEDGEMENTS

The poems in this collection have received awards in a range of national and international competitions and appeared in the associated anthologies. These include:

Aesthetica Works Creative Competition; Aileen & Albert Sanders Memorial Poetry Competition; Alpha Poetry Competition; Aural Images Poetry Competition; Barnet Open Poetry Competition; Bedford Open Poetry Competition; Biscuit International Poetry Competition; Blinking Eye Poetry Competition; Blue Butterfly Poetry Competition; Blue Nose Poetry Competition; Bridport International Writing Competition; Brownsbank International Open Poetry Competition; Castle Poets Poetry Competition; Chiltern Writers Poetry Competition; City Writings Poetry Competition; Diversity House Poetry Competition; Frogmore Poetry Competition; Hastings Poetry Competition; Kick Start Poetry Competition; Lace Poetry Competition; Lake Aske Memorial Poetry Competition; Library of Avalon Poetry Competition; Llandudno Festival Poetry Competition; London Writers Competition; Mallard Poetry Competition; Mary & Alfred Wilkins Memorial Poetry Competition; Mere Poetry Competition; New Forest Open Poetry Competition; Newark Open Poetry Competition; Northampton Literary Competition; Norwich Writers Poetry Competition; Nottingham Open Poetry Competition; Peterloo Poetry Competition; Pitshanger Poetry Competition; Poetry Life Open Poetry Competition; Poetry on the Lake Open Poetry Competition; Scottish International Poetry Competition; Segora Poetry Competition; Sheffield Thursday Poetry Competition; Slipstream Poets Open Poetry Competition; Stafford Poetry Competition; Surrey Open Poetry Competition; Ver Poets Open Poetry Competition; Virginia Warbey Poetry Competition; Wells International Poetry Competition; Writers Bureau Poetry Competition.

The poems in this collection have appeared in the following journals and publications and are reproduced by permission:

'BUS STOP'	Poetry Life (Summer 2000)
'COMMON ENGLISH ERRORS'	Frogmore Papers (Sept 2007)
'SELECTED CORRESPONDENCE'	The Month (June 1998)
'PICTURE AND POT'	Vision On (2003)
'CORRECTIONS'	The Interpreter's House (No 25)
'LOVE'	Leaf Books (Razzamatazz & Other Poems)
'INFECTED WOUND'	Frogmore Papers (Sept 2005); Tadeeb International (06)
'PERSONAL SERVICE'	The Rialto (Summer 1998)
'NIGHTFALL'	The Rialto (Autumn 2004)
'MOTHER'	The Rialto (Winter 2000)
'SUMMONS'	The Interpreter's House (Feb 2007)
'REDEMPTION'	Frogmore Papers (Sept 2006)
'THE CLEANING LADY'	The Church Anthology
'DIAGNOSIS'	The Interpreter's House (No 43)
'SEMINAR'	Poetry Nottingham (62/3)
'MRS BUNTING'	Poetry Nottingham (26/3)
'DEAR DONALD'	New Blackfriars (July/August 1997)

The poems in this collection also featured as follows:

'EMISSARY' was Shortlisted at the Strokestown International Poetry Festival 2010
'SPECIAL OCCASIONS' (as 'FINDING A CARD') was Shortlisted for the Keats-Shelley Prize 2009
'LIBRETTO' won 2nd Prize in the National Poetry Competition 2009
'THREE IN THE WOODS' received a Commendation in the National Poetry Competition 2009
'DEAR DONALD' was published in 'The Testing of Hearts' by Donald Nicholl (Darton, Longman & Todd, 1998)

I should like to place on record my grateful thanks to David Bowers and Sue Westwood, whose help. support and encouragement made possible the publication of this book.

for Gavin, Damian and Josie

CONTENTS

Bus Stop

A bus stop in Oxford Street, early morning, five of us
Suddenly a naked lady in full regalia, large swaying breasts
Slim waist and such a triangle you never saw, I gasped
A lady in a pork pie hat covered her face, the others
Unfolded newspapers or stared ahead like statues, as
She moved quietly next to me and I noticed now
A kind, pale face, perhaps distracted, and an air of
Not quite there, something weighing on her mind
Now she waited, just a touch impatiently, arms firmly
Folded, tapping her painted toe in a small puddle
Raising her hand to readjust an errant strand of hair
Gazing into middle distance from where the bus would soon arrive

So we waited, staring carefully past each other's eyes
It began to rain, and a city type eased past me
Holding out his brolly, which she knowingly declined
I've seen that one before, she said quietly to me
A girl's not safe these days, as I smiled in sympathy
Noticing the dimple on her nearside buttock as she turned
Cold morning, I said, by way of further conversation
Warm wedder comin, contributed a beaming black man
Fine by tonight, said a younger man in combat jacket
His ear-rings rattling, *yeah, could be in for several days*
As just then a bus loomed in the growing traffic and
With a sigh of communal relief we quietly jostled for position

Up it rolled, drew to the kerb, I slotted in behind her
The wheels splashed muddy rain across her thighs, and
Taking my handkerchief, with a quiet apology, I wiped
Her carefully (taking care to keep within the area affected)
You shouldn't bother, she said sweetly, *but thank you anyway*
And moving forward, raised one pretty knee onto the platform
When suddenly, shooting out across her bows, an arm
Completely barred the way, her nipples tweaking briefly
On a leather cuff. The conductor, his weasel face spiteful
With morning tiredness, spoke slowly and with emphasis
You ain't comin on my bus like that, he said
Not (the double negative betraying him) *without no clothes on*

There we stood, the rain, the bus, the hooting traffic
Five people in a line, one naked lady and a heavy silence
I think we'd be there still if suddenly she hadn't spoken
Quietly now and with a tear beginning, *I have got clothes on*
Still he barred her way. Up spoke Black Man. *Real cool gear*
He said, *de best ah've seen. Can't fault the style, straight from*
Fashion Week, contributed the Business Man. *What's your*
Problem, mate, you blind or something, asked Combat Jacket, and
Such colours, dear, you know you have an eye, smiled Pork Pie Hat
Seeing my cue, in one small second I rejoined the world
Looks fine to me, I said. He looked at us. We all climbed on
She smiled, we smiled. The sun came out. He rang the bell. And we were off

BREAKDOWN

One evening as I lay reading, the book open
on the sheets, my wife new-bathed standing near,
clothes strewn upon the bed, the evening safe
and soft and intimate, she crossed to where I lay,
her hair long and wet, the drier plugged
and ready – and faulty, as it happens.

The scream was shocking in its unfamiliarity,
high and long, the note steady in its pain,
her eyes wide and wild, the arm outstretched,
as I, in one fast movement at her side,
struck the thing from out her hand,
where it fizzed – scarring, as it happens.

Young then and careless of the precious burden
that we bore, we passed together through
babies and birthdays, joys and setbacks, the years
uncounted, until unfathomable darkness
clouded the bright eyes, breaking her spirit, and I
despairing of her state – unfaithful, as it happens.

Now, far off and separated, I hear again
the fizz, the burn, smell the tortured flesh,
the wound that warned me, a pain which now
I hold in my own hand, powerless to leave,
and longing to be where I have
no right to be – still loving, as it happens.

COMMON ENGLISH ERRORS

There's an old silver Peugeot parked in the Avenue
And, on my way to Evensong, I have to pass quite near
Seeing, in broad illuminated letters right across the back
The bold announcement *Quiksilver*. Do you follow?
Yes, without a C in *quick*, for those of you who suffered
The modern education trends and cannot spell correctly
But, in my opinion, that Peugeot and the idiot inscription
Pollute the neighbourhood, and something should be done

I mean, what mindless yob would give a name like that
To such a wreck? It's bad enough when names appear
Above the windscreen, like *Sharon and Kevin* as if we
Want to know who occupies the vehicle, who it is who
Claps the mobile to his ear as she manipulates her lipstick
And it blares its horn at me waiting at the crossing trying
To reach St Christopher's, where the Parish Council will
Find it quite impossible to start without a Chairman

On Sunday, returning home from Matins, stepping smartly
From the pavement, I moved quickly to the silver horror
And in one deft movement slapped on the windscreen my
Sticky label, ready written, with its timely admonition
Kindly respect the rules of language and observe the unvarying
Conjunction of K with C – when from a nearby house I heard
A shout, running footsteps, and Mobile Man demanding in a
Voice that never knew tutorials,' *Ere, what's your game?*

Naturally I kept my dignity, turning to face him with a
Disarming smile, and *My dear chap*, I said (determined to
Be civil), *allow me to offer you assistance. Do you realise you
Have committed a basic spelling error which does violence to
Our common heritage?* He paused, as if uncertain, and I saw my
Chance. Reaching in my briefcase, I deftly withdrew my well-used
Copy of *Fowler's English Usage (2nd Edition)*, which I always
Carry to Committee, and politely proffered it in his direction

I strongly recommend, I said, *this little book. Please accept it
With my compliments.* – But at that moment, unaccountably, he
Aimed a vicious blow, just giving me the time to raise the book
Before my face, as it, impelled by a heavy fist, collided with my
Nose. Imagine my discomfiture, the ambulance, the noisy crowd
And then the bed in hospital, where the Sister, picking up the
Blood-stained volume from my locker, asked what Fowler was
It's a defence, I told her patiently, *against common English errors*

WASH SEPARATELY

We merge
In the hot tub my sleeves swing wildly
Clutch at your lace, your lingerie, your secret silky life
In the mixed cycle
Your soft folds embrace me, brush my sad stains
And slowly your white, your virgin white, fades
Greying, in the dark washes of the night

We part
Now in a different tub my dirt dissolves alone
No more the soapy passion of entanglement
In the heavy cycle
My life turns dully, no delicates allowed
And my ugly awkward underwear vainly seeks you
Leaking, in the dark washes of the night

THE GODHOPPER

It was one of those sunny sleepy days, and
I outstretched on grass gazing dreamily at
The cloudless sky, when at my ear a small
Shrill voice protested suddenly – *Keep over,*
Move your arm, for God's sake – not what
You would expect. And so I turned, and there
A small grasshopper faced me squarely.
Excuse me, was that you I heard? I asked,

Putting the question quietly, fearing that
Some busybody would report a madman.
And it's true, a lady in a yellow dress seated
On a deck chair was looking curiously in
My direction, and calling back her children
From my vicinity. *Yes*, he said, *and don't*
Look so surprised. The last time it was human
Form, so really an insect is no big deal.

I gasped. A beatific vision here in the public
Park. *You mean you're a godhopper?* I said,
Excuse me, I meant grasshopper. That's right,
He said. *But tell me, what have you heard?*
Is the good news out? What news? I asked.
He sighed. *The Miracle at Fisons, the Feeding*
Of the Frogs, the Forgiveness of the Blackbird.
I smiled, knowing the lack of interest in

Insect goings-on, but saying nothing. *Yes,*
I thought so, he said, *another failure. I blame*
Myself. I told him, *for all the good it did,*
I might as well have been a grasshopper, and
He said, let's try it. So here I am. Theology,
Who needs it. And with that he settled on a
Nearby leaf, crossed his legs and scowled
Crossly at the birds above. *Excuse me,* I said.

I don't understand. How can a grasshopper –
But he interrupted. *The second coming. God*
So loved the world that he made his only begotten
Son a grasshopper. He thinks it's a winner. And
With that he hopped away. I looked across to
The lady with the yellow dress, now squirting
Insect spray on her protesting children, and then,
Glancing up into the boundless heaven, dozed off.

PICTURE AND POT

That morning when I woke
My wife was sleeping.
I looked at the picture and the pot
And wondered which was my favourite.

The picture
Lay flat and innocent against the wall,
A scene, hardly remembered,
Some figures, friends, perhaps laughing,
Certainly getting along, though
Not in strong colours, lying or standing,
Never changing, fixed smiles, safe,
Simply pleasant, simply there.

While beneath,
Dusty, slightly cracked, old now,
The pot, brown earth, slight smell,
And one small flower, not strong,
Striving, pushing upwards, changing,
Running a daily risk, wanting
The water which came, mostly,
And dying when it didn't.

That morning when I woke
My wife was sleeping.
I looked at the picture and the pot
And wondered which was my marriage.

SELECTED CORRESPONDENCE

Dear Maker, please find in box the product which I believe
Is yours. I have a number of complaints that I have brought
To your attention in the past, but never had an answer
(Although you say in your publicity this never happens).
Can you please review the matter? After all it's plain
Your service is at fault. This unsolicited delivery arrived
At what was actually an inconvenient time, and then
To make the matter worse, it was defective in a number
Of respects. For instance it vacillated from the outset never
Seeming set on one objective. I suggest the programme
Should be made more positive. And then there was the question
Of compatibility. It is clear the junction box is universal yet
In this case could not be connected. Regretfully and as a last
Resort I used the self-destruct facility. Does this invalidate
The warranty? There seems to be confusion on this point.
In anticipation of your prompt reply
I am, Sir, yours etcetera

Dear User, thank you for the points you raise and we

Regret that you were disappointed with the product.

First, your messages were all received and answers sent

Is it possible you overlooked them? Secondly, you raise

The question of delivery. It is our policy to sub-contract

In this respect and in general offer only guidelines.

Your third point has been carefully considered. It would

Be possible to set the programme here at source. But we believe

In the majority of cases a self-selecting programme offers

Greater satisfaction. The problem of the junction box

Relates to the original design. As fitted, it will operate

With most known makes. However, responsibility for the match

That offers optimum performance rests with the user. Regarding

Warranties, the rules are flexible and every failure is considered

On its merits. We suggest in this case that you call in person.

Wishing to retain your valued custom

We remain, Sir, yours etcetera

CATHETER

I smiled at the girl in the red dress
as she swished past the bright counter, and the child called
Mummy! and she bent in one fast move, scooped him up
in strong brown arms, pointing at fruit, kissing him,
holding him close,
and in my trousers the flat bag went *drip drip*

I stood by the door as he phoned
and asked which packet to buy, and the child in the trolley
picked up the jar, and reached it out, and stood wobbling,
and the man bent down with a quiet word, taking the jar,
settled him back,
and at my groin I felt the *tug and pull* of the tube

In the street the lights turned green
and we stepped together on the grey crossing, moving quickly,
as the small boy pulled on the pram, and the old lady
scuttled to keep up, and the lorry driver peered down
from his cab,
and at my leg the soft bag went *squish squish*

In the garden he stood with a hose
and the water pattered on the green lawn where I passed
as the small dog yapped at my feet till he called,
and I hurried, feeling it fill, the fat new weight
against my leg,
the bump and slide as it went *squeak squeak*

At my house the neighbour called a greeting
and I raised briefly my hand, pointing at the hidden bag
though the gesture meant nothing, as I hurried in,
yanked at my trousers, pulled the thing free
from my leg,
aimed the *sloosh sloosh* down as it emptied

Clothes fell to the floor, tubes dangled
And I heard the drip on the tiles, found a new bag,
fumbled the straps at my leg, swore at the fastening,
bent to attach the fresh encumbrance, staggered,
sick with the mess
and the *slither slither* inside me

Then I stood, looked from the window,
saw the brown arms scoop the child, the tot in the trolley,
the old lady nervous of traffic, the blank-faced driver,
wet lawn, yap dog, smiling neighbour,
sudden sunshine –
and the beat in my head went *life life*

AND BUT OR

I am *and* simply adding
I'm also, in addition, furthermore
For example: bubble and, mum and, love and
See what I mean? I'm good news, happy afterthought, free gift
And (there I go again) bring you bonuses
In a tacky stick-on – *and*
Of moreness

But I am *but* checking progress
I restrain, disjoint, modify
For example: everything but, sorry but, love you but
Get the picture? I'm reality, true measurement, sober reflection
And (see first stanza) cut your assets
With a tiny razor-cut – *but*
Of lessness

While I am *or* changing tack
A choice, another route, fresh options
For example: sink or, your money or, do or
You understand? I'm different, new horizons, possibilities
Or (to coin a phrase) alternivity
By a slender coupling – *or*
Of otherness

Now don't imagine (from our several voices)
That we are enemies. We work together
To make sense of what you throw at us
You have a complicated world
And it's fascinating
But it's ordered
Or it's chaos

THE LADY AND THE PASTE

It was, after all, a special day, a milestone in our
lives and deserved a special gift, so, threading
the crowds, trying, testing, alert to new things
but reverting always to the old, I spent the day
in fruitless search until, crossing the busy road,
bumped suddenly by a bulky woman, looking up
I saw, high on her coat, a flower, or perhaps
heraldic cross, my answer, the glitter of a brooch.

Small and elegant, it stood at her lapel, neat,
secure, not showy but with a certain confidence,
a fitting token of our love. And so I turned and
searched again, and found, down cobbled streets
an antique jewellers, quite empty, or so it seemed,
until I saw one small and frail old lady, grey-haired,
hump-backed, white lace at her black blouse, move
like a spider from the shadows of a dark corner.

And I described it, and in her broken accent
I hev not, she said, *but I vill find for you* and I walked
for one hour, and, returning, found her sitting back
in her corner, raising one bent arthritic finger to her
shoulder where blazed a thing of sudden flashing
lights and bright shards, a star seeming to pulse
energy in a dark sky, a jewelled miracle of light
and *Vot you vont*, she said, *you see I hev for you.*

I blinked once at the apparition, did not hesitate.
I'll take it, I said, as, with seeming reluctance, she
reached to take the brooch, looking up at me
with rheumy eyes to say quietly *It is two sousand
eight hundred pounds, she vill like it very much.*
And I paused, frozen, standing there before her
holding my wallet, shy as a bride, my words
a painful whisper, *It's more than I can pay.*

It disappeared at once, and on the counter
there was suddenly a small black box.
I sell you zis, she said, *vun hundred pounds.
It is nearly ze same. You put ze uzzer in ze bank,
you vear zis.* I opened the box. The glass eyed me
dully. I told her I would come back for the real
thing, maybe in a few years. *I am eighty six,*
she said, *I vill be dead. Do you love your vife?*

CORRECTIONS

I was reading an adventure story to my son
His face flushed on the pillow, eyes shining
When I came across this sentence
With an angry shout Jim sprang at the bearded ruffian
And stopped at once, uneasy at the situation
Who was this Jim, and why so angry, and what about the ruffian
I decided to correct it

For a start there was no place for *anger*
Certainly this Jim was upset, and no wonder
Apparently the bearded fellow was a thief
But was it his fault, and had he had the benefit
Of a stable upbringing? It's too easy
To lay blame, to judge, and this *shout* was in my opinion
Frankly, an aggressive act

I took a pencil and substituted *murmur*
Adding for good measure *gentle*, and with a reassuring word
To my son (who was looking puzzled) read aloud
With a gentle murmur Jim sprang at the bearded ruffian
But still it sounded wrong. It was that *ruffian*
That bothered me, the slur, when he was in social terms
Simply, a casualty

And furthermore to make him *bearded*

Was to demonise the fellow, when quite possibly

He had never had a bathroom. So, marking the text, I read

With a gentle murmur Jim sprang at the clean-shaven casualty

Saying to my son (now looking blank) how the text

Would thus reflect a non-judgemental attitude

Except for that word *sprang*

Then suddenly I understood

From this relationship, which Jim was starting, it was clear

He was a health professional, and the text should read

With a gentle murmur Jim counselled the clean-shaven casualty

What an improvement and all so simple

I said, reading it aloud, smiling at my son, who to my surprise

Was fast asleep

I.E.D.

'Improvised Explosive Devices, known as IEDs, are the insurgents' deadliest weapon ...'   The Times

In the dark metallic silence my clock ticks
Only the beetles and soft moths stir the dust at my feet
They pause uncertainly, swivel their lunar eyes
Brush with curious antennae the black box
Of my secret

In the packed inner space my mind works
Only the wires and tiny switches hear the hum of my labours
They click neatly, pass orders
Measure precisely the last moments
Of my undoing

In the still air my heart bursts
Only the heat and charred walls remain of my lodging
Fragments journey, take routes
Reach blindly the blood and brick
Of their resting place

In this happening I am fulfilled
No thought or feeling mars my perfection
Safe in my purpose I have no morality
Free from the terrible burden
Of my maker

CENTURION

Stand to attention.
I don't want to hear this kind of complaint,
Especially about a Centurion.
I know it happens with new recruits,
Well, it's not a pretty sight, takes some getting used to.
But a Centurion …
Look, stand at ease, take your helmet off.
You've seen plenty of action,
This is a shock.

Take a seat on the bench.
I don't want the men to hear about this,
It's bad for morale,
And there's already a lot of unrest.
It's been a long tour of duty, we're all feeling the strain,
But you're a Centurion …
Maybe a spot of leave, the baths somewhere,
You've earned it,
Give yourself a rest.

Get up off your knees.
You're off duty pending leave.
Look, it's not our business,
Religion is for the priests.
It doesn't matter whose son he is, he broke the law,
And you're a Centurion …
No, I don't need forgiving, and nor do you,
And joining his lot,
It's out of the question.

You're confined to quarters.
No, no communication with the men.
If you go public,
It's out of my hands.
As things stand I can hush it up, your record is exemplary,
A first class Centurion …
But we can't go round forgiving enemies,
Think of the Empire.
Leave your sword there.

A Kiss at Dying

The screen was blue
As they bathed me and the pain ached in my side
But I remembered a blue dress
And the ponytail bobbed as she ran
In the bells and the buzzers and the hurrying feet
There was only a garden and light laughter and
A tiny hand claimed mine firmly
As feet skipped and slowed and finally she reached
For the arms that took her to bed
And I saw the white walls of the corridor swim past
And the gates of the lift clanged shut, but I sensed
Her kiss lay on me like a blessing

Their caps were green
As I lay on my back and started the count they wanted
But I remembered games
On the green lawn and the clack of mallets
In the bright lights and the murmurs and the mask at my face
There was only her quick dart under covers, the dolls gathered
As she asked for the stories I told
Stories she knew and stayed always the same
Like petals she kept and pressed in her memory
Miming the words, the parts I would play
And the needle slid in my hand and I felt my eyes close, but I believed
Her kiss lay on me like a blessing

The dream was deep
As they went to work and the black pump breathed for me
But I remembered the sand and the shore
And squeals on sharp stones as little legs raced for the sea
In the cuts and the scalpel and the dark butchery
There was only the sand on her toes, and sleepy eyes
As she laughed at the end of the story I told
Then her arms reached up, circled, pulled me down
And they saw the breath falter, paused, raised hands from the wounds
As she smiled, pursed her lips, leaned to me
When the pain dulled all at once and the world slipped away, and then
Her kiss lay on me like a blessing

EMISSARY

In the Honey Islands, across the Bogo River, a shy people give guarded
welcome to genuine enquirers into their gentle life-style, lining the bank
and offering flowers, garlands and bracelets of local berries, while never
touching or eating which are private activities among families seen only
by close relatives and never by outside visitors.

Verbal communication is limited to the absolutely necessary, open
gestures preferred to the spoken word, and rituals of thanks, promises
and apologies enacted in small groups which cluster excitedly whenever key
events are heralded by stamping of feet and raised arms, signals which bring
witnesses to the square round which dwellings are grouped.

Dress is minimal, unnecessary clothing considered aggressive, though
face-masks are de rigueur and visitors are often disconcerted by the freely
displayed genitalia carefully coiffured and emphasised by strokes of
bright pigment indicating age and family, facilitating easy recognition from
childhood through to old age and infirmity.

Marriage is carefully managed through monthly *Ambulations*, when
concentric circles of the young are rotated simultaneously in opposite
directions according to gender to the sound of flute-like wind instruments,
while families sit observing to one side, indicating with smiles and nods
as choices become apparent and couples detach from the ceremony.

Fidelity is paramount, the *Unified Ones* moving to new huts and maintaining
life-long mutual commitment through feasting and procreation, though the care
and education of offspring are shared by the wider family and young couples
play a leading part in dance, celebrations and hunts while taking their turn with
any necessary supervision of the young and old.

The language is simple and not difficult to learn based on simple statements
round common objects, the question-form possible but regarded as hostile,
the imperative never heard, the subjunctive non-existent, words in general
considered dangerous and even destructive, abstract nouns such as *beauty* and
love existing in grammatical form but never spoken.

Religious practice is uniform, the central figure of *Ugar* dominant
but never mentioned except as a quiet utterance in difficult times or as a
cry of joy when babies arrive or enemies sheath their swords, illness, accidents
or natural disasters met by quiet smiles or on occasion a mysterious and
beautiful circling gesture linking earth and sky.

Death is a joyous event, celebrated by the entire family of the
Transcended One (as they are called) who greet the *Atoners* (those who
have offended him during his life) ceremoniously accepting their symbolic
offerings of honey-smeared knives which are then used to decorate in
ornate patterns the faces of surviving relatives or friends.

I returned home after three months in the Honey Islands, bearing the
characteristic marks, laden with gifts of honey wine in ornate oval pots
fashioned from dried bark, but without my research assistant Albert who
on the last day left the hut in jeans eating peanuts, kissed our young host
goodbye, asked the nature of *Ugar*, and whose throat they cut.

FLASHPOINT

I was moving past the plate-glass window, lost in thought,
as she appeared, drape-laden, pins held from out her painted mouth,
and bent towards the naked manikins, enclosing them
with practised ease, when, from her half-unbuttoned blouse
there dropped, in sudden wondrous fall, one perfect flawless breast
and hung there, poised and pointed, stilling me where I stood.

I gasped, then in an action all unconsidered, moved closer,
smiled, and motioned in an open gesture my quiet admiration
for her youthful beauty, while behind me I heard the steps
of passing shoppers pause, as she stood up, and, in a movement
quick and graceful, with one hand gathered up the errant orb,
restoring it to its enfolding lace and secret modesty.

Still I stood, when suddenly, even as I smiled my approbation,
her cheeks now colouring and pins flying from her open mouth,
to my amazement she bent her head towards the space between us,
making with her slender finger a gesture whose import had
but one meaning, and in a voice which even in that busy street
sounded through the heavy glass, *Piss off!* she loudly shouted.

I turned, hearing now the muttered comments of two lady shoppers
who had placed their loaded baskets on the pavement, and, arms folded,
surveying me with scarcely veiled contempt, were conveying
to a quickly gathered crowd my crime and evil ways, as I, moving
past them before the threatened call to law enforcement could
be made, fled the scene, chastened, abject – and not a little thrilled.

LOVE

To find me, follow the main B road out of
The city centre. You come to a roundabout
Which you leave at whatever exit. Take the
Path of least resistance, and keep off the
Beaten track. Disregard local signs. Beware
Dangerous loads and expect a roundabout
Route. Allow for delays and diversions.
Take a bearing on the furthest point and
Go past the spot where the birds sing. You
Should see a cow in the field on your left.
Turn into the hidden drive, and look for
The old door with no key. Let yourself in.
I may be there, or possibly not. Make yourself
At home. You're not expected.

THE WATER LILY

Today the water lily bloomed.
Shyly, with just a touch of the coquette,
she reached fingers to her green bodice,
glanced sideways, toyed with me, affected not to know,
as I, crouched shirtless at the water's edge, voyeur,
ventured closer.
Then, promptly at eleven
(the busy gnats couldn't believe it),
the small pink bud went topless.

There was a sudden hush.
It was a sensation and she knew it.
She did a little half-turn as the water rippled,
then lay flat on her back, glowing pink.
I straightened up, stumbled and stepped back, captive,
couldn't take my eyes off her,
my camera taking pictures by itself
(it was all you could hear in the silence).
Oh you fireball, you gypsy you,

wide open and shameless,
flaunting it and didn't care,
you could see that centre stage was all she knew,
pushing up rosy red softness, there in broad daylight,
reckless who saw, reached out or touched her, wanton,
while the wasps flew small crazy circles,
and I told her she was mine
(not quite true but I was her lover)
and she was my universe.

It couldn't last.
By mid-afternoon the show was over.
She took a couple of bows, then got dressed,
the long curved stalks drawing her down into the dark,
and at the same moment the sun dipped and went out. Curtains.
I called her name over and over
as the flies buzzed and the gnats hovered
(even the water skater did a couple of turns),
but there were no encores.

Just another affair.
It was bound to end badly.
They all said she wasn't right for me.
But I'll always remember the way she stood, just out of reach,
then suddenly gave it all, lovechild.
I long for her
on still nights when I lie sleepless
(her red kiss poised over deep water),
and tears come in a hot rush.

HOSPICE

Surely, though in my body old,
and dying,
yet not daring to be told,
slowly and in pain I ease the knot
to loosen where the bonds withhold.

Gratefully, though former doubts withstand,
and praying,
yet now my prayers unplanned,
firmly and in faith I bend the knee
to all I cannot understand.

Gladly, though with no eyes to see,
and happy,
yet not hasting to be free,
at last and inwardly I turn the page
to delve the deepest mystery.

Finally, and with a settled mind,
though missing
all I leave behind,
in death I meet my love's embrace
to furnish all I could not find.

MY PANTS

Suddenly your pants have steel inside them
Well thank you very much.
I'm not sure if steel would interest my wife at this stage,
but all the same the message left on my computer
gives me hope that somewhere in the new world
salesmen have my interests at heart.

But let me advise, here's the message that
they should be sending:
Suddenly your pants have self-cleaning properties
That would interest my wife at once,
underwear that cleans itself, no yellow stains,
that she can safely wash among her own.

And another message I'm still waiting for:
Suddenly your pants have in-built kindness
which would lead me uncomplaining
to garden chores, washing up, remembering
all birthdays and rousing me from drowsy TV afternoons
to undertake the jobs long listed.

And as an extra they could offer:
Suddenly your pants reject all violence
instilling patience, ready forgiveness, a desire
to right past wrongs, showing charity
towards old enemies, and understanding
rival claims to land and liberty.

I long to see the final message:
Suddenly your pants discover life's true meaning
open you to love and laughter, fill your time
with cherishing the gifts you have, and from
the sleazy web of lies and fiction
reap a richer harvest.

INFECTED WOUND

Albania 2005

It lay in the huddle of grey blocks
Where the mission stood, and litter spilled
Down the dirt track. It creaked in the rust
On the hinge of the gate that the simpleton
Opened for us, shone in the mud on the shoes
Of the nuns as we followed their steps.
When I turned in the iron bed to the wall
That night, the boxes stacked on the shelves above
I could read in the scrawl by the fading light:
Infected wound

It beat with the drum of the two blind men
Who moved down the street, and the crowd
Parted before them. It clung to the lips
Of the gypsy boy who pushed his hand
In the car, snarled with the one-eyed dog
That circled the shoes of the man who phoned.
And it gleamed in the eye of the legless man
Who begged in the square as he raised his stumps
From the dust and called his cry:
Infected wound

It ran in the walls of crooked bricks
Of the mountain huts, and old men trudged
In the rain. It scratched with the hoofs
Of the tethered cow that blocked the path
To the crest, and followed the pointing stick
Of the peasant girl who showed the way,
Touching the group who carried the sick child
To the church, and was there in the soft sigh
As the needle slid in the thin arm:
Infected wound

It was there as we left for the airport road
And lurched in the ruts, and the fan stirred
The dead air. It walked the tarmac
Smelling the oil and jumped in the dust
Of passing feet, clung to the plastic tag
On the case declaring its right to leave.
And it watched from afar the waiting plane
Which I took as I turned and left at last
For the easy lies of the life I led:
Infected wound

A Note From Prague

Mickey,

Turn off the gas

Before you go in the kids' room.

They should be OK but Jamie had a fall at school

And may need cheering up. Sharon is in a state about

Her party at Sarah's tomorrow, so make sure you get her dress

From the cleaners before they close.

Your mum

Called this morning

I tried to do what you told me

But it was really difficult. I don't know

Why she hates me so much, I do try. It's not true

About airs and graces, I've always wanted to write about

How I feel, even before we were married.

The class

Is only once a week

And it's not your darts evening.

It's nothing to worry about, just ordinary people

Who write about what happens to them. And the tutor

Says I have a talent. When we were paired up for an exercise

I was with someone who had been to Prague.

The notes

You found were about our life

And what happened to us. I know you were angry

And it should have been private. But I thought if I could write

It down, maybe you would understand. It was going to be a poem

That's why I couldn't tell you before, and I needed to get away somewhere

Or I'd never be able to finish it.

The old city

Has cobbled streets

And if you walk over the bridge at sunset

You can see turrets and towers, and all the civilisations

That ever lived there, and it's a completely different language.

I should have told you I was going, but my sister took both the kids

And anyway I phoned so you needn't have worried.

I tried

To explain this morning

When I got home, but you wouldn't let me.

It was like being in another life, the sort of place

I want to be forever. And I couldn't tell you about the poem because it

Wasn't finished. But now it is, and I hope one day you and the kids will read

A Note from Prague

REDEMPTION

That day I wrote an extra Christmas card for the window cleaner
Apologised to Jasper for dragging him past the lamp-post
Said Good Morning to mad Mrs Calthorpe instead of crossing the road
And put out three old shirts for the Oxfam bag
Then I took ten Panadol with a double gin and tonic
Brushed my teeth and turned in
Everything seemed in order as I closed my eyes
But I still woke up the next morning

The next day I kept below thirty as I drove through the town
Asked Henry if I could help fix his mower
Discussed the good news with two black callers selling Watchtower
And sent off fifty pounds to the Peruvian orphanage
Then I cut my left wrist with the big kitchen knife
Ran a hot bath and lay back
Things were fine for the first half-hour
I spent the rest of the evening in Casualty

In the morning I wrote to my old uncle in Australia
Talked with Albert for an hour on a prison visit
Gave my lecture on Civic Responsibility to the WEA
And saw the solicitor about a new Will
Then I rigged a makeshift noose from the loft trapdoor
Stood on a chair and stepped off
It held for a minute or two
Until I hit the floor with a nasty bump

On the fourth day I telephoned my ex-wife
And asked her to forgive me for the divorce
Wrote three letters to the children apologising for what had happened
And explained to Sheila that it was all over
Then I took down the old shotgun from on top of the cupboard
Slid in a shiny red cartridge
Pulled back the ancient rusting hammer
And finally had a good night's sleep

NIGHTFALL

I have made my bed,
Spread the sheets and tucked in the sides.
The blankets are neatly folded and all's well
In the quiet, still bedroom where I will lie
In the darkness, total darkness,
Windows wide to the night sky,
Tasting the thick, sticky air of absence.

Don't disturb me,
Don't check to see that I'm all right.
Forget me, have your supper together
In the hot kitchen where I cooked,
Loved to cook, with the noisy pans
Hands in the blood of the meat,
Turning the dirty pages of the old cookbook.

Make your beds too,
Find a room that honours you.
See that you brush your teeth,
Don't even think of staying up late.
Outside the wolves will gather as one pack,
But you have no need to worry,
Easing your tired body on the old springs.

The day will dawn,
There's no secret about it.
At the window an old woman will cough,
Dogs will bark and hurricanes will take place.
But your bed will be comfortable,
The sheets dry as dust,
Spreading out the white flag of surrender.

PERSONAL SERVICE

I went in to buy a pair of socks (brown, no pattern, foot size ten)
And wandered about, bright lights, big hall
Two people bumped me, a small boy said stupid old fucker
And I lost my shoe when a pram came from behind
(They have to be wool, regulations)
So I went up to a girl in a green blouse
That said Vera on a badge just above her left breast
And asked her to give me a hand
She said she was on cash and they didn't do personal service
But the appropriate aisle was over there on the right

At menswear socks and underwear (Y-fronts, jockey shorts, athletic)
I found a selection, three ranks, plastic bags
They were on a long rail, and when I looked for my size
The seven packets in front all dropped on the floor
(Mine have got holes but I wear them as long as I can)
A lady in a white coat said you're having a bad day dear
And I told her it was a whole lot worse at Cassino
But remember me to the folks back home
Then I used the cover of the dress stands with their thick foliage
To work my way past the snipers and over to Pay Here

I told the girl sitting at signals (tired eyes, plumpish, no cap)
That I had a girl, childhood sweetheart, name of Vera
Used to live here, but we got separated, end of leave
I still carried her torn photo in my fag tin
(Unless they're thick your feet bleed on long marches)
She said straight off that she'd talk to her superior
So I settled myself on the leather seat of the dug-out
Took a bit of care in reconnoitering the surrounding terrain
And checked over the plastic bag of field rations
You can't be too careful in no-man's-land

It wasn't long before the officer came (young, posh voice, desk wallah)
Looked me over, talked a bit about conduct, asked for I.D.
I told him he wanted to get to the front more often, look after the lads
We'd seen too many like him
(It was insubordination all right but I'd had enough)
He just stood there in the open, give him his due
No cover, didn't turn a hair, they were moving in from all sides
I told him to keep his head down, he went on about socks
What a time to think of welfare
Any other time that's the mark of a good officer

In the end they had to pull us out (shouts, bells, flanking movement)
The poor devil just cracked up, went gaga, flipped
Under a strain, I grant you, but didn't see the guns
I had to drag him down under cover
(Only a packing case but blended in well with the surroundings)
Even then he didn't see the danger, wanted to fight back
Strength of ten men, clear case of shell shock
All the while I could see Vera watching, tears of pride
We'll meet again, I said as I heard the rush of feet
We'll meet again some sunny day

SPECIAL OCCASIONS

I hurried into the shop and made my way to the section
where they kept Special Occasions. I looked all through
the labels – Leaving, Bereavement, New Job, Driving Test –
but it wasn't there. *Excuse me*, I said to the young assistant,
as she finished arranging cards in the appropriate slots,
*I wonder if you can help? I've got this friend who's just been
sent to prison. Do you know if you have anything suitable?*
She smiled sympathetically. *We may have something,* she said.

We walked to the back, and she pulled out a heavy drawer.
What about 'We'll Miss You', she said, *or even* (she smiled gently)
'New Home'? I bent down and started sorting through, just as
a man standing near us edged over. *Could you help me find
something?* he asked. She turned to face him as he paused.
I had an affair, he said, adding quietly, *it's over now.* I saw
her reassuring smile, as gently she led him past me, reached
upwards to a shelf. *There's simply 'Sorry',* she said, *or do you*

want a fuller message? What about ' I'm Such A Chump'?
Would that apply? I saw him smile and take the card, but just then
they were interrupted by a girl in jeans and grubby tee-shirt pulling
roughly at her arm. *Look*, she said *it's a message for the kids I want,
two boys, one girl. They've gone away.* The young assistant handed
her a tissue. *Don't worry*, she said, *do you miss them? Is it a school
trip? What about 'Have Lots of Fun'?* The woman shook her head.
No, she said, *you don't understand. I've lost them. They're In Care.*

38

The young assistant smiled brightly *Right,* she said, taking
her hand, *something cheery is what you need. We'll have a look,* as
just then a bearded man butted in. *My brother left his kid with me,*
he said, *to babysit … I messed with her. Do you know what kind
of card would do for that?* His eyes lowered as she moved closer.
Let's see what we can find, she said, *where do you want to start?*
She pointed down and as he knelt to reach the lower shelf, I heard
her read the cards' inscriptions. *What about 'Can You Forgive Me?'*

she murmured, *or perhaps* - he looked up at her - *'Words Are Not Enough'?*
Her hand touched his shoulder. *Find one that fits,* she said, *you choose.*
Just then I was aware of someone darkly-suited standing at my side who
seemed to be in charge and was watching happily. He must have read my
thoughts. *She's a godsend,* he whispered, *never fails. There's nothing she
can't cope with.* Glancing round, I saw her take her coat and move
towards the door. As she turned to join the busy crowd outside, I caught
a final glimpse, seeing now the streaming tears which marked her face.

PAINT POT

I was perched on the topmost rung
When it fell,
Toppling off the platform,
Bouncing down the side of the ladder,
And spinning upside down for a further few feet,
Before splashing its contents
Over my marriage.

It caught the corner of the shed
Where the affair began,
Running down the windows
That I had covered over,
Coating the carefully locked door.
And leaving a puddle
That my children stepped in.

It spattered the climbing frame
And the swings,
Even the little wooden horse
Got covered.
Hopscotch nativity play school reports
Birthdays and anniversaries,
All dripped with it.

It fell clean through the divorce
Still spinning,
And a great slew of red
Splashed across two families.
Universities first jobs grandchildren
Had a flat grey wash
That nothing would remove.

The ladder stands at the top window
As I look down,
And at the bottom
The paint pot lies out of reach.
Hazardous, it says on the tin, Keep Sealed
And I remember
The colour of happiness.

THE GARDEN VISITOR

One morning as I stood quietly by the garden table
Crusts in hand, savouring the breeze and watching
The small birds peck and squabble at the crumbs
I scattered there, I heard at once a sudden firmer
Flutter as a small grey elephant, dapple-winged
Legs creased and leathered now gently extended
As they braced for landing, settled there before me
And was still at last, resting on the dewy lawn

He stood, sides softly swelling from his exertions
As the worn wide ear flaps fanned a cooling rhythm
I smiled in rapt appreciation, watching his skill, as
Tired from his flight, with a wistful air he delicately
Pushed and probed his subtle trunk among the daisies
Searching for the morning feed I tossed towards him
And with a sideways glance seeming to acknowledge
My quiet presence and the morning peace we shared

So he softly grazed and as I reached slowly my hand
To touch and stroke his leathered side he moved as if
In modest deference his large and lofty bottom
Sideways from me and with a slow and measured tread
Rounded his bulk until he faced me squarely, all the
While his large eye holding me steady in a gaze which
Seemed at once all-knowing in an ancient wisdom
And yet childlike in some secret rumination

Now as the wind grew strong he raised his trunk made
Damp with morning dew upwards to test each shifting
Change and then in soundless strength, wings beating
Steadily, the grass about him flat in mute obeisance
He lifted gently from the ground, hung hovering there
For one long second, balancing his poised mass against
Each ebb and flow, then of a sudden swung upwards
As the stronger draughts reclaimed him

And as he moved on spread wings steadily into the blue
And distant sky, turning once his great head back towards
The tiny garden, I saw his trunk briefly extend and as if
In salutation or perhaps farewell wave once before he passed
Beyond my sight, and, as I settled at the garden table where
The still unfinished breakfast brandy bottle waited, I paused
And silently gave thanks, rejoicing that our God all-wise
Should thus create a being so majestic in its daintiness

LOST BALL

Beyond the flag,
buried in weeds, a lost ball,
stained, chipped, a long abandoned thing.
I bent to it,
we laughed together.
It was usable,
not for real,
not for the match,
I told her I'd use it for practice.

Between tee and green,
walking, casually, soft evening light,
sleepy almost, the words dreamlike in the still air,
I heard myself say it.
Out of nothing,
no question asked,
no prompting,
I turned and said it.
The trouble is, I love you.

In the silence,
turning quietly, looking at me,
loving almost (but not quite), smiling,
she said it.
You can't, don't.
No blame,
no outrage,
she stopped and said it.
If you do, you'll spoil everything.

In the clubhouse,
drinking, seated together,
the weight in my pocket reminded me.
On the table,
she held it,
her fingers
were deft.
I tossed it in the bin.
It bounced once and was still.

LADIES

I'll be a few minutes, she said,

wading out past the reef, and stood,

her smile seraphic as she turned to me,

holding a graceful pose, arms akimbo,

her hair a golden halo against the bright sky,

and her eyes bright with merriment,

as, beneath, the hidden stream ran

into the forgiving waves of the blue sea,

and all the little fishes ran for cover.

AFFAIR

As I opened the drawer
It sprang at me
White, frothy, lace-saturated
It beckoned, smiled, lured, suggested
Slithered out, ran up my legs
Behind me the mirror
Held me in frame
I felt the full gaze
On me stooping
I looked behind

I gave in and posed
In the way I knew
Long, lean, a real coquette
I smiled, turned, twisted, pouted
Moved round, stretched my legs
My lover couldn't resist
Found the right angles
Raised me on tip-toe
Engulfed me
I whispered yes

Now I was wanton
Walked barefoot
Strutted in the hot room
I was glam and gorgeous, prey and predator
No-one could have me, anyone could
I was drawn, held close
Clung to, pressed with cool lips
I kissed back
And we both understood
I said now

As I closed the drawer
The room darkened
I gathered the scattered clothes
Dressed, tidied, opened
The curtains to the dull day
The mirror watched, kept silent
Made no comment, accepted the grey figure
Swallowing
My secret
Deep inside

MOTHER

Driving through the city one hot June,
I saw, through the open window
my dead mother,
walking, smiling at me,
hand raised briefly,
lost in the crowd then seen again
among the pavement's shapes,
my own mother walking slowly,
waving to me,
and her gone these twenty years.

Pulling to the side, I turned in puzzlement,
looked back, searched the passing figures,
my living mother
I saw her, the shuffling slippers
turned outwards on the dusty street,
bent forward, her hands arthritic
on the wheeled basket's broken handle,
smiling, nodding as she always did,
talking to everyone,
and her bent fingers beckoning.

Leaning across, I reached my hand towards her.
There she was, moving slowly,
my own mother,
but no nearer, her hands tucked
in the apron's grubby front,
holding pegs. Now washing flapped,
I saw the frying pan, smelled herrings.
Where's your coat, boy
You'll catch your death
Her head rocked back in laughter.

Calling to her, I pushed open the door.
She turned from the sink, one leg bent up behind.
It was my mother,
the grey hair wispy, the plate of mince set down,
adding the shopping bill with broken pencil stub,
losing her glasses, stumbling on painful knees.
These stones need boiling, I heard her say.
Now at the fire, knees apart,
cars were hooting,
still she chattered at me.

In the dust behind I saw her.
She waved smiling,
my mother.
She turned away, the small round back towards me,
as on the wind I heard familiar words,
As you go through life
I drove on,
the mirror bright,
the facing traffic blurred
in tears.

SUMMONS

Dear Sir

      I regret having to address you
In this impersonal way. But please understand that times
Are difficult. War and pestilence were not expected
On this unprecedented scale, and our resources are
Severely stretched.

      I am writing to inform you
That your time has now expired. You are expected to report
To this office within the next day. You should look for
The New Arrivals sign, quoting this reference as
Your authority.

      It is understood
That you profess a formal faith, and have expressed concern
At an unprepared departure. It is not our policy to extend time
For acts of penitence, which in any case have no force
In this office.

      Following your reception
You will be shown to Dispersal, where you will be allocated a
Provisional location. A final judgement will not be made until
All relevant parties have testified. This may necessitate
A considerable delay.

I am not at liberty
To disclose full details. But I am allowed to state that
In your case the testimony to date is contradictory.
Several persons have spoken in your support. They are
In the minority.

We are concerned
That others, known intimately to you, have suffered through
Your acts. There is a prima facie case that you did not take
The opportunity to use your gifts in charity. This charge is one
You will be called to answer.

You are not permitted
To divulge the contents of this communication to anyone,
Including the hospital authorities. If you have questions or concerns
Regarding these arrangements, please speak to me in this office
On your arrival.

Yours faithfully
Administrator

CALL-OUT

I was sitting in the theatre when suddenly the call went out,
Is there a poet in the house? And I shook my head in disbelief,
The one evening when I was off-duty, and someone had to
Lose faith. I stood, moved to the corner where the crowd
Had gathered and pushed my way through. *Thank God,* one said,
It looks serious. I bent to where the young girl sat motionless,
And saw it in her eyes at once. *The heart's broken,* I said,
And she's losing dreams fast. Does anyone know her?

A man pushed forward. *She's my partner,* he said,
She's had these turns before, no-one can explain them.
I bent again to the young girl and saw her eyes close.
Can you hear me? I asked softly. Then I turned to face them.
I'll do what I can, I said, *I've got one or two hopes in my bag
That may keep her going until we can restore full belief.*
Just then a large man, in formal dress, appeared behind us.
Will you take her somewhere? he said, *we've got a show to run.*

We walked her to the foyer and she sat, still silent.
In a quick couplet I raised the prospect of ease and plenty,
And for a moment she rallied. But she needed something stronger.
Only metaphysics could help her now, and in that public place
I had no specialised equipment, nothing to revive the vital signs.
But she was dangerously short of joy and I saw I had no option.
I took a risk and gave her the works – purpose, meaning, love,
A sonnet, no preparation, delivered where she sat.

The girl's partner came forward and knelt beside her.
She's not responding, he said. *Wait,* I said, *give her time.*
We waited. The eyes flickered open. Almost imperceptible, there
Was a tiny smile. *She's recovering,* someone whispered to me.
No, I said, *just stabilised.* The man stood up and faced me.
What do I do now? he asked. Behind us we heard raised voices
And applause as the show got under way. *We're missing the start.*
I stood up. *Take her home,* I said. *Find a different show.*

PRAY

She was smooth black svelte
Shone mauve from head to toe
As I looked from the gleaming polished shoes
To the black suit, the dark-hued chiffon scarf
And her face, red-lipped, smiling in repose
The eyes mocked, half-hidden, behind the shades
And her hair glistened, swung at her shoulders
As long fingers, thick silver bands shining
Moved slowly against the white page
Of the book held loosely there

It was bright, crisp, new bought
Gleamed its title as the page turned
Urging its importance, a shrill command
In massive type *Think And Grow Rich*
And what I couldn't understand, what snagged
What drew me back to stare and stare again
Forgetting the passing stations, stuck fast
In the mystery drama of this other life, was
The leather bookmark flat on the white page
Which said simply *Pray*

RED ROSE

I turned in to Rose the Florist

And went to the counter

Listen, I said, *I'm in dead trouble*

The tarty one came over

We've got carnations, she said, *nice white ones*

Three fifty or choose your own for a fiver

The schoolgirl helper smiled at me

Depends what you want, they have different meanings

The fat lady in the cardigan was writing bills

No credit cards, she said

I walked over to the display

It's not just a birthday, I said

I want something serious

The tarty one examined her nails

Has someone passed over

You might do better with an arrangement

The schoolgirl helper picked up some flowers

Lilies are nice for bereavements, how about pink

The fat lady in the cardigan sipped tea

We don't deliver, she said

I went to the window

You don't understand, I said, *I hit her*

We had an argument

The tarty one chewed her gum

Can't think of nothing for that, she said

Don't often get asked

The schoolgirl helper put down a blue bouquet

That's not on, she said, *violation of rights*

The fat lady in the cardigan wiped her glasses

We close at six, she said

I sat on the sill

Jesus Christ, I said, *this is it*

It's the end

The tarty one was putting on lipstick

I expect she asked for it, she said

She'll come round

The schoolgirl helper put on her coat

Compatibility, she said, *some people just don't have it*

The fat lady in the cardigan touched my shoulder

A single red rose, she said

PORN

Kurt pulled back
Sorry, he said, *give me a minute*
Christ, said Cara, *we've only got two days*
She stood up and pulled the robe round her
The bald man sat down heavily on his chair
The two technicians turned to each other smoking
The tea girl went round collecting cups
No one spoke

The bald man walked over
Kurt was sitting by the imitation pool
They told me you were good, he said
I haven't got all day
Kurt was staring at the backcloth
He knew that if he looked at the bald man
He would strangle him
He didn't move

A technician offered him a cigarette
Nice scene, he said, *reality*
I like the way you bent her over
They like it rough
Kurt moved away
He wanted to throw the technician through the wall
Wipe him out
He closed his eyes

Cara sat next to him

She was applying lipstick as she spoke

Listen, can we get on with it

I'm on a tight schedule

I don't know what your problem is but

Any way you like just say

Think of the money

Kurt didn't look at her

The tea girl tapped his shoulder

Would you like a coffee

I don't know if you're allowed, it's my first day

I was wondering if you'd give me a lift after

Save my bus fare

By the way I'm Anne

Kurt looked at her

Up he came

THE CLEANING LADY

He asked me to sit down
And sat quietly opposite
We had plenty of time
And I looked behind him to
Four pins and a matchbox on the dusty shelf
One dead fag end in the fading sun
And a single rose in a broken jar

There were always two sides
And I had to see it differently
We had some time
As I stood and touched
Four pins and a matchbox on the dusty shelf
One dead fag end in the fading sun
And a single rose in a broken jar

It was a question of rebuilding
And it wouldn't be easy
We had a little time
As I made a pattern of
Four pins and a matchbox on the dusty shelf
One dead fag end in the fading sun
And a single rose in a broken jar

What about next week
But now he had to go
There would be more time
As I put down
Four pins and a matchbox on the dusty shelf
One dead fag end in the fading sun
And a single rose in a broken jar

Could she come in
It was time to do the rooms
And in one move
Swept up
The pins and the matchbox from the dusty shelf
The fag end and the rose and the broken jar
And the hurt and the pain and the next appointment

Pro Patria

It was the flank of the forward trench where
he stood, braced against the mud wall.
Duck-boards slid under his clogged feet
as he stooped, hearing the sudden call,
and the whizz-bang crashed somewhere behind,
when the voice he knew, that voice, the one with the cane,
Hold on, it said, *'B' Company is relieving you.*
There was a pat on the arm as it passed.
I hope so, he said.

It was the third bed on the left where
he lay, hands gripped on the side-rail.
The cough rattled his aching head
as he reached, fumbled for the tin cup,
and spat and spat again, called out in fear,
when the voice he knew, that voice, the one with the pills,
Get it all out, it said, *I'll be along in a minute.*
There was a pat on the leg as it passed.
I bloody hope so, he said.

It was the second long trestle table where
he waited, holding his Record of Service.
His bare feet slipped on the wooden floor
as he bent, signed the green form,
took the hat and the shoes and the suit,
when the voice he knew, that voice, the one with the tie,
You'll be all right, it said, *there are jobs lined up.*
There was a pat on the back as it passed.
I fucking hope so, he said.

It was a flat on the ground floor where
they found him, huddled in an old armchair.
There was a blanket round his shoulders
as he sat, not wanting to look at them,
taking a sip of the tea they offered,
when the voice he knew, that voice, the one with the notes,
Don't worry, it said, *we've got sheltered accommodation.*
There was a pat on the head as it passed.
Fuck off, he said.

INNOCENCE

Oh the thrill of it, the fun of it
As she ran teasing past
Tossing her tail, her pig-tail
Urging me, goading me
To run, jump, catch
There at her blond head
The sign, the silky sign
The thick plait
Of her girlhood

Oh the love of it, the joy of it
As she swirled by
Swishing her skirt, her pleated skirt
Telling me, daring me
To dart, lift, see
High over her bare legs
The badge, the unseen badge
The white knickers
Of her mystery

And the shame of it, the hate of it
As she stood and wept
Wiping her eyes, her lying eyes
Blaming me, accusing me
Of hurt, harm, dirt
To Miss Willis
The judge, judge and jury
On the unclean mind
Of my boyhood

And the face of it, the fear of it
As she pointed the long nose
Knitting her lips, her tight lips
Bending me, slapping me
On my thighs, bare thighs
Of my pulled-up trousers
Teaching the truth, the bad truth
Of all the women
Of my future

LIBRETTO

The heroine lay dying in her pasteboard cot
Seized by coughing, clutching with both hands
The big tenor who knelt at her side
It was too much
I slipped from my seat, stumbled through feet and knees
Mounted the stage in a burst of saving love
For heaven's sake, I said, *she's a sick woman*
An attic is no place for a consumptive
They hustled me to the wings

She took the stage, flaunting her gypsy skirt
In a fast spin, taunting with jutting hips
The workers who crowded close
I saw the danger
Hurried down, pushed aside the protesting musicians
Climbed the steps in a last bid to stop the brawl
Calm down, I told them, *love's all right in its place*
But there's no need for knives
They escorted me to the foyer

He reached out, touching the breasts of the peasant girl

In a sly gesture, reassuring her

He was a rich man, her key to a new life

I was disgusted

Stood up, decided to give him a piece of my mind

Burst out in a last attempt to protect her virtue

Come off it, I shouted, *we all know what you want*

Take your hands off that poor girl

They marched me to the door

Outside, I saw the bus, splashed through driving rain

Slipped in a puddle, fell heavily on the oily road

Under the big Jag, which screeched to a halt

I gathered my senses

Sat up, heard the chorus of concern

Broke into song in an effort to find the key

Take it easy, they said, *the ambulance is here*

This is no time for singing

They cut short my aria

ABLATIVE ABSOLUTE

I still remember the light blue grammar,
the tiny tear of pages opened, ever since
it followed me everywhere.

But one thing, one page
that never left me, the day he said, *Today,*
we take the Ablative Absolute,

and you, he said, *translate the first line.*
And I did, and there it was, the sense sprang out
With the tribute having been paid -

Yes, he said, *with the tribute having been paid,*
Caesar departed. And the neatness of it, the nerve,
the taking for granted

took my breath away, and still does.
Ablative Absolute: time or circumstances attendant
upon a main action, I love it still.

It's a construction, I told my wife
as we lay in the hotel bed, whispering at her later
With the seeds having been sown, she slept.

Look, I told my children, *you can say*
so much with so little, with the sentence having been started
Laughing, they loved it too.

With my daughter having been married,
I told them at the wedding, as they smiled at my speech,
I can enjoy retirement.

And all that world around, I ordered,
tidied, rearranged in clauses, parsed and conjugated,
learned it from the light blue grammar.

Now it takes another meaning.
In the hospital my wife sits at my bedside as I murmur
With the tribute having been paid, I depart.

EVENING STANDARD

When I decided the other night
to make love to my rather bored wife,
just as I was making preliminary advances
she picked up the newspaper,
and as I started to get into my stride
turned to the inside back page
and started reading out Cooking Tips.
The key to soufflés is whisking the eggs, she said.

I was in no mood to comment
and continued with normal business.
But as I was warming to the task
there was a rustle as she turned over the page.
I decided to maintain a discreet silence,
not wishing to interrupt her train of thought,
but she suddenly found the Weather Forecast.
Showers moving in from the west, she said.

Things proceeded quietly for a while
until the Competition Corner caught her eye.
She took down a big atlas from the shelf
as I made minor adjustments to accommodate,
and started looking up the population of Honduras.
I'll need a calculator, she said, *it's in the drawer,*
and I passed it to her with my free hand,
taking care to leave the other one in place.

As I settled into a comfortable rhythm
she turned to the Crossword
and reached for a pen on the bedside table.
I did my best to avoid unnecessary commotion
in order not to disturb her concentration.
But as I was getting into the swing of things
8 letters, she said, *starts with F, means happiness.*
Foreplay, I grunted, out of breath.

By this time I was nearing my destination,
but she suddenly looked round tiredly
and asked if I could expedite matters.
I knew she wasn't interested in the Sports Section
so I told her I'd do my best and she folded up the paper.
But at the last minute as I craned my neck forward
and bellowed, I just caught a fleeting glimpse of
the winning goal in extra time.

THREE IN THE WOODS

In the woods she skipped at my feet, swung on my arm,
pestered for stories, as the dead leaves drifted down,
and my wife, thoughtful, slightly apart, walked ahead,
when my small daughter looked up to the high branches
and pointed suddenly to the black bird which swooped
clattering, from the bare tree-top, wheeling across the
dark clouds, as she jumped for joy and tugged my hand,
and I lifted her in my arms, shouting at the sky
Mrs Big-Wing has gone shopping! and my daughter
clapped her bright red mittens, and laughed aloud.

On the path we slid in the wet mud, splashed our boots,
as her mother, ahead, touched the oak and wandered
alone between tall trees, when before us, a squirrel
paused, eyed, picked up a nut, then rounded the trunk in
a grey flash and I took the hand of my small daughter
and we followed him laughing round and around,
as she splashed for joy through the brown puddles, and
her giggles echoed in the dark wood as I called out
Mr Humbly-Grumbly's gone for his supper! and she
whirled the red mittens in two bright arcs at her side.

On the bank we slipped on the damp grass and slithered
into ferns and wet bracken, as far off the lone figure
turned and watched unmoving, and I waved while we
stood and wiped the caked mud from our coats, when
I saw, motionless, not ten yards distant, one forepaw
raised, the thin red fox peering through leaves, and
I hushed my small daughter and motioned, as he silently
slunk back, and her eyes widened and I whispered
Mr Slinky-Pants has seen us! over her muffled squeal
as she held one red mitten over her open mouth.

By the lake we stepped carefully to the edge and watched
as we saw the thrust of tiny flippers, and a green frog
darted like a spear below us, and my daughter called out
beckoning to where her mother stood like a statue
on the old wooden pier, and gazed out into deep water,
and did not turn or move, as my small daughter looked
back to me with the question unasked in her eyes, and
I drew her back in my arms and said softly to her
Mummy's talking to God, and she pressed to her cheeks
the bright red mittens, and began to cry.

RETURN VISIT

The donkey's head drooped as we climbed the track
To the little dusty inn. Around us the stony desert
Stretched out, darker now and colder as night fell.
A boy took the donkey and I called for the innkeeper.
I won't be staying long, I told him, *but I've called*
About my friend. Well, not exactly your friend, he said,
And we both smiled. *Did the money hold out?* I asked.
We needed extra bandages, he said, *and then he got*
An infection. I reached down to my purse. *No,* he said,
No problem. He's still here, by the way.

I walked through to the bar and looked round. It was
Crowded but he was sitting on his own, in the corner.
There was a big swelling over his left eye, his arm
Was strapped across his chest (probably the one they
Broke when he tried to defend himself), and some
Sort of crutch was leaning against the wall. There
Was a jug of wine on the table. I slipped along the
Bench next to him, and there was a kind of rustle of
Disapproval round the room. I poured wine for both
Of us. *How are you feeling?* I asked.

He looked round at me. His eyes were dark, hard
To see in the candlelight. He pushed away the wine.
Are you feeling better? I asked again. He looked round
The room, keeping his voice low. *Thanks for helping,*
He said. *I thought* - he paused - *I thought I was a goner.*
The innkeeper slid into the bench opposite. *How's the*
Patient? he asked. *Stay for another couple of days, make*
Sure you're strong enough. He reached over and patted
Him on the shoulder. *Take the lower road home,* he said,
Keep out of trouble. We all laughed.

Suddenly a hunk of bread came flying though the air,
Bouncing on the table and knocking over the wine.
I picked up the knife. The innkeeper touched my arm.
Then he stood up and turned to the other tables. *Listen,*
He said, *anyone who doesn't like it here, they know what*
They can do. No one spoke. He sat down, gestured for
Another jug of wine and started mopping up the mess.
He raised his cup to us. *All the best*, he said loudly.
We raised our cups and drank. There was silence
In the room. We sat and waited.

THE OLD MRS TWEED FEELING

It was a poor sort of place, a dump school, just outside the town
Deserted by all but no-hopers, brutes or oddballs
And I spending one term there, just a job
Before moving to higher, better things. For years it was
A fund of dinner-party anecdotes:
I was once at this school ...

He was just another teacher, taught Geography, I think
Tall, balding, nothing special, not someone you'd notice
Drove a small car, never spoke about his wife.
His life began the third week I was there, when
It happened, Mrs Tweed arrived
She was absolutely gorgeous ...

The angel, as we came to know her, slim, blond hair
With a mischief in the deep blue eyes suggesting
Bed, or bath, certainly some place where
Clothes would play no part, but laughter would.
I simply shared the nudges and the winks
But Mr Morton had glimpsed heaven ...

He didn't stand a chance, maybe even knew it, but tried.
He opened doors, carried her books, made sure
She got her coffee, even changed her wheel
Looking stunned when once she smiled at him.
But it would never be enough
He had to take the step ...

It was the letter that did it, he left it in her pigeon-hole.
I'd do anything, he wrote, just give me a chance.
She showed it to me, asked me to have a word,
I went to his room, heard him crying, and turned away.
We never saw him in the school again
Well, what would you have done?

I looked on Mrs Tweed with wonderment, not lust or longing.
I had my own angel then and could laugh at his infatuation.
Some say he had a breakdown, others that he topped himself.
Now, crossing aged knees as skirts fly past, yearning and alone
I know his moment and
I never tell that story any more.

DIAGNOSIS

That morning my wife levelled with me
We thought it better not to tell you
It explains those headaches you've been having
It's Parabolic Dyanide Spondosis
There's no known cure
I sat up in bed, rearranged the pillow
And turned to her
I thought as much, I said, let's face this thing together
It's cold outside, she said
I think I'll wear my beige

She opened the wardrobe door
You'll find it difficult, she said
But at least we know those nightmares when you
Clambered on the roof and sang
Were just a symptom
And when you had that awful wind at Pamela's
We were puzzled at the time
But now we know it's normal in the later stages
The pelezoid attacks the gronge, she says
Would you pass that hanger

She put the suitcase on the floor
The treatment isn't easy, she said
Twice daily injections in the lower contribule
I don't know how you'll reach
Without my help
Apparently libido is a telltale sign
I thought so, I said, I should have known
It's why I fucked that statue in the cemetery
They called today, she said
And asked for compensation

She turned at the door
I'm spending the week with cousin Joan in Cardiff
If there's anything you want
Phone after six, try not to make a fuss
She's been unwell
There's morphine in the fridge
And don't forget the undertaker's booked
For ten tomorrow, tell him the hymns you've chosen
Look at that rain
I'll catch my death

She closed the door
I turned in the bed and switched on
The Hallelujah Chorus, poured a double gin
Opened a box of truffles
And ran a bath
Then I rubbed myself all over with body oil
Changed into yellow silk pyjamas
And phoned the doctor
Pam, I said, she bought it
We've got seven days

CROSSROADS

The sun lay heavy on the hard ground
And the jeep
Like a lost toy, tiny
In the vast terrain
Ahead, a deep gash in the rocky track
Beyond, the road led on
No way through, they said
Crossroads
We sat silent, hunched in the shade of the open door
Dust, sand, oil, hung in the hot air
And the sweat on our faces
Heat pressed

We drank water from the open packs
And I stood
I'll try, I said, *have a go*
And looked at the gap
It was deep, jagged where the earth had split
To the side a tilt of rock led through
The angle's impossible, they said
Crossroads
I sat in, started the engine, inched forward
Rocks and rubble crunched under the wheels
Halfway - and it hovered
I stopped

My son climbed to where it perched
And touched my arm
Let me do it, he said, *my turn*
And I stepped down
He sat inside, they watched as I shook my head
The engine roared and rock crumbled
Go for it, they said
Crossroads
He went for it, in a rush, fast, fearless it seemed
Stones, sand, grit, leapt from the spinning tyres
It lurched - bridged the gap
And braked

The door opened and he smiled at us
I sat suddenly
Well done, I said, *we're over*
And they started clapping
He walked to me, *You did the first bit,* he said
And I remembered my hands, tying his laces
You did the last bit, I said
Crossroads
We drove on, they were noisy now, making their plans
Danger forgotten, and, quiet in the back
I was letting
Him drive

IRREGULARITY

He leaned forward in his chair.
How often does it happen? he asked.
I thought for a moment, then realised it was pointless
trying to count the number of times.
So I said *Quite often,* and waited to see
what he would make of it.

He pulled a pad towards him.
Is it always the same thing? he asked.
Again I paused, then decided it was worth telling him
the kind of things that did it.
Sad things for example, I told him,
like when my mother died.

He smiled at me.
That's perfectly normal, he said.
I looked at him, knowing he was doing his best
to keep me from worrying.
But happy things too, I added,
happy things in particular.

He tapped his pen on the desk.
I don't quite understand, he said.
There was a pause, and I went to the window
looking out over the paved entrance.
A young family turned into the drive
and I watched their progress.

He put down the pen.

We don't have unlimited time, he said.

I saw the mother take the boy's hand gently,

murmuring something as they reached the door.

Behind them the man swung the little girl in a wide arc

as she squealed *Daddy!*

He stood up suddenly.

These are not serious symptoms, he said.

I joined him at the door as he opened it.

Look, I said, *the love, the trust, it's unbearable*

The tears streamed down my cheeks.

Possibly some irregularity in the tear-duct, he continued.

SEMINAR

Years ago the Master had written *Words and Things*,
A kind of treatise, part philosophy, hugely influential
In its day, my generation's heritage, we talked of little else.
Where was it I first turned those pages, in a packed
Tutorial, lying wine-happy on a summer lawn, or buried
In some soundless library? At the first discussion I waded in,
Shouting down the others, ripped up one girl who failed
To understand the argument and saw her in tears. Later
I had tea with him, and his wife took me aside. *He likes you,*
She said, *but wonders why your words are weapons.*

He looked at me as I entered the room. The others
Were silent. Beyond the window the lake glistened.
Take loving, he said, as I sat. *Love, loving, lover,*
What's the difference? I hesitated. *We love,* he said,
And may at times be loving. He paused. *But lover,*
He concluded with a smile, *means something more.*
He tossed the essay across the desk. *Tell me,* he said,
Do you think, are you thinking, he stopped smiling,
Or are you a thinker? I picked up the essay.
This is shallow stuff, he said, *where's the heart?*

I always meant to stay in touch. Years later
His wife telephoned and told me of his stroke.
She took me to him. He sat, bent like a twig, folded
Into striped folds on an old deck chair next to roses
And protective thorn. He looked up. Those eyes which
Once chillingly had pierced when I advanced a sloppy
Argument wandered vacant and confused to where I stood.
Does he know me? I asked her. *Just talk to him,* she said.
It really doesn't matter what you say. I turned to him.
I'll leave you, she said, *you need some time together.*

I found a chair and sat beside him. *I'm glad to see you,*
I said. *I meant to write.* He stared at me. *All my life,*
I said, *I've felt you there. I owe you everything.* Still
He said nothing. Soon she came back and fussed over him.
I think that's enough, she said, *he mustn't get too tired.*
Have you had a pleasant chat? I stood and moved away.
She turned to me. *Why are you crying?* she asked.
I bent down and picked up the fallen rug,
And wrapped it carefully around his feet.
I'm sorry, I said, *I'm a crier.*

MRS BUNTING

When did you call, Mrs Bunting
With your shopping bag and references
Standing in the rain, Mrs Bunting, dripping from your red mac
In my littered porch
What did I say, Mrs Bunting, how did you cope
With the booze and the rudeness, smiling your smile
As I staggered and fumbled
Finding a day

When did you enter my house, Mrs Bunting
With your shiny cans and yellow cloths
Seeking out the dirt, Mrs Bunting, moving tables and chairs
Never touched
When did you first come, Mrs Bunting, with your chat
And chiding, clearing the mess, shelving the books
Except one you brought on
Starting Again

When did you clean the stove, Mrs Bunting
Scrape the grease from the sticky top
Open the door, Mrs Bunting, push your pink gloves
In the black pit
When did you pause, Mrs Bunting, when did you lean
Over the old chess game set out on the dusty desk
And enter your sharp move
Knowing it won

And the bathroom, Mrs Bunting, when did you
Plunge in the dark loo
Turn things white, Mrs Bunting, bend your round back
Sleeves rolled
And the singing, Mrs Bunting, what made you sing
When you brought me tea, urging the time, handing me clothes
Had me blinking and angry
Facing the door

Somebody phoned, Mrs Bunting, I was at work
Board Meeting, Minutes, Conference
You wouldn't be coming, Mrs Bunting, did I know
Would I like to attend
At the funeral, Mrs Bunting, the priest said nice words
How you were cheerful and kind, the usual things
I stood up and left
Discovering my love

WHAT ALFRED IS

I met Alfred
Alfred is a burglar
But *is* he?
I mean, is he a burglar only when he burgles
Or all the time? When he smiles at his children
For example, is it a burglar smiling, or only
Alfred? In other words, it's the burglariness
Of Alfred which worries me. Where is it, is it
In his eyes, his hands, his mind? What does it
Consist of? Or is there no such thing? Is it only
His profession which he follows intermittently?
Is he a burglar, for example, inside the house
At night, in a striped jersey, carrying a jemmy
Which he then discards and isn't a burglar once
He's home in bed? But then, what happened to
The burglar that he was? And in any case must
You do it well to qualify? Could you say, he's
Not a real burglar because he burgles badly?
But that would make nonsense of the statement
We were burgled by a bad burglar, which alas
Makes sense. And this habit that he has, taking
Things at night from other people, was it born
In, does he have a burglar gene, or was there
An Uncle Bill to teach him from an early age?
Again, does wanting come into the question?
I mean, could Alfred overcome a lack of talent
By his application, not aspiring to Burglar of
The Year but achieving entry to less prestigious
Houses? Of course, this way of looking at the
Question may be wrong, and burglarhood is
What we should consider, a status recognised
By training and examination, leading to eventual
Dip Burg. I asked a philosopher about these
Questions and we discussed ontology. But
It's not ontology that bothers me at all, only
What Alfred is. And if you wonder why I'm
Bothered, it's what happened when I met him
Alfred is a burglar
And he asked me
If I'm a poet

DEAR DONALD

for Donald Nicholl
(1923-1997)

Dear Donald
These are the words which you would not let me speak
When, in that room, back bowed, for once
Cut low from those aspiring heights where always I had seen you
You summoned me for our goodbyes
And, as I struggled with the love and thanks which rose
Together in one breath for one to whom I owe so much
Your gaze, clear and steady as it always was, and your quiet words
Stilled me, seemed to say
As in all things the natural time will come

And so it has
Now, from four corners of my life, the memories return
How once, years ago, I walked with you, skipping childlike at your heels
As the long strides outpaced me, down a leafy lane
And, dazzled by the moment, giddy with ideas and tumbled thoughts
I spilled my noisy mind to your patient ears, heedless, veering on and off
The straight path you trod, with my oft-repeated *What I really think -*
And stepped before a car, and you, reaching out
Plucking me easily back, *Be careful of the road,* you said
Or you'll not think at all, and in that moment seemed
To anchor for a lifetime my scholarship in sense

In those years
I wondered why you spurned what I most prized, as, ever distrustful
Of the picked argument, the need to conjure things from words
You headed off my clumsy overtures with *Is it warm today?* and
Would you like some tea? to bring me from philosophy to something
Nearer home. There, your children, lifted high and laughing on your shoulders
Saved you from such deceits, and farmers they would be, and foresters, you said
Yet, as I left, casual-seeming and with a smile you gave a compass-bearing
Have you read such-and-such? you said, and closed the door
And left me in unfamiliar silence, stopped the hard hammer of my mind
And instead, and for a lifetime, set seeds growing

Years later
Your loyalty undimmed, the letters with their "peace and love" neatly inscribed
The conversations, slower now, and the writings with their subtle patterns traced
Were landmarks in a far country. Then as the loss, bitter and haunting, struck
At my life, we met again, as if you sensed when to replenish where my life's spirit
Sweetened by your company, had drained. And there you sat, fresh from preaching
Holding the table's fond attention, gently mimicking, your eyes twinkling
With some mischief story as I came late to join you, and turning, asked me directly
How my loss had come. Now there were no words, just my pain and silence as
You watched, and then said simply *It happened*, and in that steady gaze freed me
Showing, for a lifetime, how to keep safe a private grieving

In later times
I saw you less, but still we talked, and I could see always in my mind
Your tall back, venerable as oak, arched down to the enquirer, your eyes sharp
Heard still in your voice, quavering now, the hesitations longer, the words elusive
Your kindness and concern, the old fastidious taste for truth. Now again my life
Took fresh paths and uncertain I sought your help, expecting after so many years
A token offering. And yet you called, wrote letters, tested my resolve
Giving the spur I needed, yet obliquely, as if we worked together for the aim
So that I never felt the debt, until that day when, taking your leave, touching
With a smile the lofty plans and purposes, *It will be exciting for you* you said
Setting me joyful, leaving a lifetime's inspiration

Dear Donald
These are the words which you would not let me speak
Which, in that room, you saw was not their time
These are the lessons which I learned easily in your company
But never knew till later I had learned them
These -- the commonsense that walks with intellect, the gentle nurturing
Of thought, the glad acceptance of love and loss alike
And the courage to learn and move on - these were the gifts you gave
Which I could not tell you as you died, and here today
These words, and thanks, and all I touch with them, are yours